Sahmad Nakumbe's Strategies To
Growing Your Business Online!

How to Increase Your Revenue Online!

Sahmad Nakumbe's Strategies to Growing your Business Online! How to Increase Your Revenue Online!

Library of Congress Cataloging-in-Publication Data
     Nakumbe, Sahmad
          Sahmad Nakumbe's Strategies to Growing your Business Online! How to Increase Your Revenue Online

ISBN-13: 978-1530108022
ISBN-10: 1530108020

1. Business & Economics / Marketing / General
                    First Paperback Edition Revised 2016

LEGAL NOTICES

The information presented herein represents the view of the author as of the date of publication. Because of the rate with which conditions change, the author reserve the right to alter and update his opinion based on the new conditions. This book is for informational purposes only. While every attempt has been made to verify the information provided in this book, neither the authors nor their affiliates/partners assume any responsibility for errors, inaccuracies or omissions. Any slights of people or organizations are unintentional. You should be aware of any laws, which govern business transactions or other business practices in your country and state. Any reference to any person or business whether living or dead is purely coincidental.

Every effort has been made to accurately represent this product and it's potential. Examples in these materials are not to be interpreted as a promise or guarantee of earnings. Earning potential is entirely dependent on the person using our product, ideas and techniques. We do not purport this as a "get rich scheme."

Your level of success in attaining the results claimed in our materials depends on the time you devote to the program, ideas and techniques mentioned your finances, knowledge and various skills. Since these factors differ according to individuals, we cannot guarantee your success or income level. Nor are we responsible for any of your actions.

Any and all forward looking statements here or on any of our sales material are intended to express our opinion of earnings potential. Many factors will be important in determining your actual results and no guarantees are made that you will achieve results similar to ours or anybody else's, in fact no guarantees are made that you will achieve any results from our ideas and techniques in our material.

Acknowledgments

Believe in yourself and your abilities.

Gratitude to…
My Family & My Mentors

TABLE OF CONTENTS

PART ONE:
The Beginning:
Knowledge To Maximize These
Marketing Strategies

PART TWO:
Business Strategies To Generate
More Sales and Increase Profits

PART THREE:
Online & Internet Strategies That Generate
Tons Of Prospects And Customers

PART FOUR:
Publicity Strategies To Get Your Name
Buzzing At Little To No Cost

PART FIVE:
High-Powered
Marketing Strategies

INTRODUCTION

I f you have been in business for longer than two minutes, I'm sure that you have already stumbled across something that completely surprised you and instantly opened your eyes to a world of new possibilities. Maybe it was a brand new salesperson you just hired who went on to break every sales record in your company within their first six months. Maybe it was a vendor who sold you products at prices so ridiculously cheap that it allowed you to sell the product at bargain prices and still allowed you to actually make a few bucks. Well, no matter what the event was that opened your mind to new and exciting possibilities, the fact is that you were shown indisputable proof that more success and profits were possible than you had previously believed was possible.

This book that you hold in your hands is more of that indisputable proof. So, if you are willing to read this book with pen and paper in hand, while keeping an open mind, then a business-changing revelation is exactly what you will experience today. Not only will you will find yourself believing in your business again if you have had minor setbacks, but you will reawaken the excitement and joy you felt years ago when you first realized that having your own business could provide you with the freedom to create your own life and future.

Now, I realize that I am making a big claim, but as you turn the pages of this book, you will see for yourself that these proven success strategies really can increase your profits. In fact, the strategies in this book are quietly being used by successful businesses all over the nation to make them large fortunes. The real tragedy is that most business owners are too stuck in their old and unprofitable ways to embrace the changes in the marketplace that lead to real profits.

However, I don't want to sugarcoat the reality of what will be required for you to reach a much higher level of success. ALL of the strategies in this book will require you to make changes in your business. In fact, you should only be reading this book because you are ready to implement new but proven strategies to reach your desired level of success and profit in your business. First, let me give you a piece of golden advice. In order to implement the strategies in this book, you must to let go of every belief that doesn't directly contribute to you depositing more profits in your bank account. Many times in the past I've been hired by business owners who have many beliefs that are slowly but surely draining their bank accounts. That is why the first chapter of my book is geared towards preparing your mindset to make more money. So, without further adieu, let's get started on growing your business.

PART ONE:

The Beginning:
Knowledge to Maximize These
Marketing Strategies

CHAPTER 1

Get Your Head in the Game

Preparing your mind for success is the first step on the path to extreme success in your business during this new economy. In fact, I'll even go a step further and predict that unless you address your mindset first, you won't even implement a single one of the proven strategies in this book.

Think it sounds a bit harsh? Well, would you rather me sugarcoat it and skim over the meat and potatoes or would you rather sit down and get a seven course meal that will have you bursting at the seams with ready-to-buy, customers and profits?

See, the truth is no matter how great the strategies are that I reveal within the pages of this book, you will never see one extra penny of profit, unless you are willing, ready and able to make the changes required. And that, my friend, requires guts, boldness and the ability to move rapidly to follow the money in your local market.

Let me give you few examples of how powerful and profitable OR how broke and hungry a mindset can make you. There's a successful furniture chain in New England which promises delivery in 3 days or less. Do you have an idea of the average amount of days or weeks a customer was accustomed to waiting to get their furniture delivered before this company decided to re-write the rules? Normal wait time was three to six weeks for in-stock merchandise. In fact, I would venture to say that 95% of the furniture industry still requires customers to wait two to six weeks for delivery. This furniture store has a huge competitive advantage over every other competitor in the marketplace.

Now, before this furniture chain came to the area, no other stores were delivering furniture to a customer's home within a couple of days. Do you think these owners were scorned and warned by ALL the other furniture retailers who they asked for advice? Do you think manufacturers, vendor reps and delivery companies scoffed and swore that it couldn't be done? Of course! See, every furniture store has the same problems and objections as any other furniture store, but the owners of this furniture chain believed that they could do it better and faster.

The owners of that company had the iron resolve of a bear. They had a powerful mindset that allowed them to grow beyond belief...during a RECESSION! However, they first had to change their mindset BEFORE they could ever change their business. That's what you will also have to do in order to grow your business to the next level.

Now, let's look at how badly things turn out when business owners have a stubborn and poor mindset. Several years ago there were several super-high end furniture stores within miles of each other in New England. These retailers were priced so high, that only two percent of the population in the entire nation could afford their furniture. As the economy turned, those retailers simply refused to change their business model to reflect the change in the economy. Therefore, within six short months ALL but one of those retailers went out of business.

Unfortunately, the stubborn and poor mindset also affected many other businesses who could have easily weathered the storm of this economy with just a few simple changes to their businesses. However, they chose to ignore the changing marketplace and consequently went out of business.

So, now that you know how powerful a mind-set change is to your success, let's look at four powerful keys and realities that you must embrace in this new economy:

1. **Accept that there's still money in your local marketplace.** Don't feed me that garbage that people in your area aren't buying the type of products or services that you offer. Yes, they are. There are dozens of businesses who are making unbelievable profits during this recession. The real question is, "Will yours be one of the businesses that will make the necessary changes in order to cash in during this economic period?"

2. **Take advantage of the opportunities that recessions create.** Every recession creates an opportunity for someone to profit. In the example of the furniture store chain that I mentioned earlier, consumers want furniture that can be delivered quickly. The customers in that market don't want to wait for months. They want good prices, speed and convenience. Ultimately, the key to your success will be determined by your ability to listen to your market. Then, all you have to do is create a product or service to meet that need and you'll instantly have increased profits.

3. **Make decisions based on facts, not news headlines.** If you're listening to talk radio, news reports and any other media source that's pumping fear, doom and gloom into your head, then turn it off right now! The majority of news media sources are in the business of selling fear, not hope. Your focus should be on finding what your target market wants and then giving it to them at a great value. That's it. Don't let the media drive you out of business, by slowly draining away your will to fight.

4. **Change your business or go out of business.** Every day I meet so many business owners who simply refuse to do things differently, but yet, they expect different results. That's the textbook definition of insanity. You must be willing to change your staff, advertising, marketing, product and/or management, and any and everything else, in order to survive during this economy. That's the truth, plain and simple.

CHAPTER 2

The Four Keys to Explode Your Business via a Marketing Plan

While preparing your mindset to go to the next level in your business is the first step towards transforming your business into a marketing machine, there are several other key principles which will also impact your success. These four key factors are so important to your business success in this economy, that unless you build your marketing strategies using them, you will have a 99% chance of failing. So, take your time with these four cornerstone principles and then implement them into your business.

Key #1: Calculate the Lifetime Value of Your Customer

When business owners hire me to help turn their business into a money-maker, one of the first things I do is calculate the lifetime value of their customers. The lifetime value (LTV) of a customer is the amount of profit each customer brings to your business over the course of their buying lifetime with your business. Now, I will show you a simple way to calculate the LTV, but unless you keep great records you should probably hire a bookkeeper to dig through receipts and calculate the numbers for you.

In order to help you calculate your lifetime customer value, I will give you an example below.

Total Amount of Customers for the year	100
Average # of purchases per customer	2
Average Purchase Amount	$125.00
(100 x 2 x $125) **Total Revenue**	**$25,000.00**
Cost to produce each product or service (including parts & labor)	$35.00
Total cost to produce product for the 100 customers *(100 x $35)*	$3,500.00
Marketing Costs for the year	$5,000.00
Total Costs	**$8,500.00**
Total Revenue - Costs = Gross Profit *($25,000 - $8,500)*	**$16,500.00**
Gross Profit	$16,500.00
Customer Lifetime Value For The Year *($16,500 / 100 customers)*	**$165.00**
So, in this example on average each customer represents $165 worth of profit.	

So, in the example I used above, when someone buys from that business, on average they represent at least $165 in profit. However, it doesn't have to stop there. In fact, your goal should be to increase the lifetime value of each customer by getting them back into your business to purchase from you more often.

The reason why the lifetime value of a customer is so important is because it gives you an idea of how much you should invest in marketing to get the customer in the first place. So, in the example above the business owner knows that if he spends another $5,000 in marketing in the same ways he's investing in marketing now, he can reasonably expect to double his profits. Without knowing the lifetime value of his customers, he wouldn't have the confidence to make that kind of investment in marketing.

Key #2: Find Out the Source of Every Lead That Comes Into Your Business

If there was one piece of advice that I would want you to remember from this entire book, it would be tracking where every lead comes from that you get into your business. In order to track where your leads come from, you can ask prospects when they walk into your business or you can use special phone numbers with unique extensions in your ads. You can also use five page websites designed for a specific sale, coupons, tracking codes or anything else you can think of know exactly where your prospects are coming from.

At the end of the day, you absolutely need to know exactly where your leads are coming from, so that you can know exactly what's working in your business. Once you know where your leads are coming from, then you can begin to invest marketing in those specific areas that are generating the best leads and customers. Without tracking your leads, you will always be wasting thousands of dollars on ineffective marketing strategies.

Key #3: Calculate Your Return on Investment for Any Marketing That You Do

This crucial key builds on the previous key that I mentioned. Quite honestly, the only way to truly know your return on investment is to track the results of every marketing strategy. Once you know how much you are spending, then you will know exactly how much each marketing dollar is bringing back to your business.

For example, if you spent $500 on an ad in a local newspaper which generated two customers, who then spent a total of $3,500 in your business, your return on your investment is 700%! So for every $1 you spent, you received $7 back. That's a very good investment by my standards.

Key #4: Create Ads And Marketing Materials That Consistently Put Money In Your Pocket:

If you ever want to see a huge waste of money, then watch the ads being played during the Super Bowl. Those ads that run during the Super Bowl ads are designed to be funny and cute and win advertising awards. However, those ads rarely make their companies any real profit. As a matter of fact, those commercials are the laughing stock of the marketing industry because companies blissfully line up and pay millions for those types of "funny" ads while receiving little to no results for their marketing dollars.

The fact of the matter is, you either need to know how to write and design good ads or have the resources to hire a good copywriter. Regardless of which option you choose, I encourage you to study good copywriters so that they have a feel for what usually works. As the owner, you should definitely know how to create ads, letters and emails that generate leads. A good expert to study to learn copywriting is Dan Kennedy. Simply type in his name in Google.com and you will find tons of resources about copywriting.

Here's a quick tip sheet on the basics which every ad you create should have:

1. Use headlines that attract customers.
2. Always have a compelling offer.
3. Use a specific start date and deadline in your ad.

4. Insert testimonials from past customers.
5. Include a guarantee on your products and services.
6. Your ad must look unique and stand out from your competitors.
7. Your ad must ONLY focus on what your customer wants.
8. Have only one goal for each ad, which is to get customers to visit your business.
9. Tell the reason why you're offering the sale.
10. Write ads that are straight to the point and easy to understand.

Now, the keys to success listed above may seem like a lot of hard work, but you only have to do the hardest work in the beginning. However, the most important factor which will contribute to your success in your business is your willingness to actually implement these strategies on a consistent basis.

CHAPTER 3

Business 101: You Must Constantly Advertise Your Business!

Sounds obvious, doesn't it? But, you wouldn't believe how many business owners I've met who refuse to do any type of consistent marketing or advertising! That is unbelievable to me; however it is normal for many businesses. The following statistics give you a glimpse of how people are using the Internet to find the products and services they need:

- 64% of U.S. Gross Domestic Product comes from local businesses.
- 4.2 million local small businesses have sales in the $500,000 to $20,000,000 range.
- Over 1 billion local searches are performed monthly — a number that grows more than 50% each year.
- 98% of searchers choose a business that is on page 1 of the results they get.
- 41% of clicks go to the #1 ranked site in a search.
- 12% of clicks go to the #2 ranked site in a search.
- 8.5% of clicks go to the #3 ranked site in a search.

These statistics show how important it is for your business to develop and implement an online marketing strategy to get your business to the top of the search engine results so when prospective customers go searching for you (without knowing your name or business name) they find you.

Sure, they will do a small little ad in the local newspaper once or twice a year, but that can hardly be considered marketing. Sure, you don't market or advertise your company and you have people coming through the door. My question for you is, are you at your goal? Do you have the maximum amount of clientele coming in? Then why aren't you marketing your company? If you are the owner of a local business, you are probably suffering from a drop in demand for your products or services as a result of the economic recession most areas have been suffering from for the past few years. In fact statistics show that small local businesses are making 30% to 50% less than they were just a few years ago.

If I were to ask you what kind of business you're in, what would you say? If you're like most business owners that hire me, you would probably just pick a product or service that you sell and simply tell me that you are in that industry. Right? Well, I'm here to tell you that your answer to the question of what business you're in, *should* be, "I'm in the marketing business." If that was not your answer, then I already know that you're most likely having huge profit problems in your business. Many business owners are confused about what business they are in. The simplest way to look at your business is to realize that the two most important activities in your business is marketing and actually providing the product or service that you're marketing. Every day that the doors of your business is open, is a day that you should be focusing on marketing.

Over the years, I've come to the realization that most business owners are not to blame for not being able to put together effective marketing campaigns. Think about when you first started your business; did you receive an instruction manual about how to get customers? Was there a course offered down at the local college designed to teach business owners how to attract quality buying customers? Heck, no. You just went out there and told everyone what you're doing now and then you probably sat back and waited for customers to come into your business. If that was not the case then you pushed the opening of your business via word of mouth. Back then things were pretty simple and easy. However, that gravy train didn't last, did it?

Next, you probably turned to the industry publications, magazines and newsletters, which focus on products and customer service as the solution to your problems. So, over time you looked around at what the competition was doing and you probably began to think that if you also offered product or service at a lower price, customers would flock to your business too. But, is that what happened?

Maybe at first you saw a rush of customers the first time you ran a new ad or promotion with the product at a low price, but did it continue on like that? No. Then, as time went on you probably began doing less and less advertising because you weren't seeing the results from you advertising dollars. But deep down inside, you knew that you had to do some type of marketing and advertising, but you had no idea what to do. After all you're a business owner, not a marketing and advertising guy.

That is where you're terribly mistaken. See, if you want to be a *successful and profitable* business owner, you MUST become a marketing and advertising guy! Your number one job every single day is getting more customers into your business. That's it. Why, you ask? Because the only way you make money is if prospects come into your business and are willing, ready and able to pay you money in exchange for your product or service.

You don't get paid to counsel employees, do payroll, answer questions about when the delivery truck will arrive and you sure as heck don't get paid to sit around all day waiting for someone to walk in. You only get paid if and when a customer pays you. So, your number one job every day when you wake up has to be getting more paying customers through your doors. The only way to do that is to become a marketing and advertising fanatic.

When you begin to look at yourself as the marketer of your business, instead of just a business owner, it will become very easy to see if you're doing the right things to attract customers or not. I knew business owners who NEVER advertised their business and shortly after the recession hit, those guys went belly-up.

In fact, every day that you seriously want to make money, you should be running a different promotion, ad or marketing campaign. Don't tell me that customers get tired of seeing your ads, because I'm going to tell you to advertise in a different area that hasn't seen that specific advertisement or promotion yet. Don't tell me that it's too expensive, because I know about one hundred ways to advertise your business on a shoe-string budget and most of them cost less than what you spend on lunch for the week.

In order to succeed in this new economy, you MUST view yourself as the marketer of your business and NOT just an owner of a business.

CHAPTER 4

When Everybody Is Your Customer, Then Nobody Is Actually Your Customer

One of the biggest challenges business owners must overcome in order to be successful in this new economy, is the dreaded "I-offer-everything-for-everyone" syndrome. On the surface this seems like a sure way to get more customers, but it's been proven time and time again that it's not always the most successful way to prosper for 99.9% of businesses.

If you're a small business owner, then chances are that you have a limited budget and limited space to work with. So, let's say for example that you're a furniture store. If your store offers several contemporary collections, several ultra-modern collections and some eclectic pieces as well as some early American collections scattered throughout you business, do you really think you have enough of any single style to satisfy the type of customer who's looking for a specific style? The answer is most likely no.

In fact, the most successful furniture retailers in my area focus on a couple of things to attract a specific type of customer, such as:

- Complete living room packages for under $2,000 or furnish your entire home for under $5,000.
- Long-term low or no interest financing
- Fast delivery within 3 days or less
- Lower prices for packages

So, by narrowing down their advertising, they attract the types of customers who purchase multiple pieces, which in turn, drive the average ticket sale and profits up. They then offer generous financing terms, which attracts customers with good credit and income, while enticing them to spend more money because the customer has longer to pay for it. Most importantly, the successful retailers in my area price their sales so that the more merchandise the customer buys, the bigger the discount the customer receives.

There is also another twist to these retailers. See, although they attract customers to their business with generous financing offers, they reward their salespeople handsomely for NOT selling the long-term financing, therefore giving their salespeople an incentive to get customers to pay off their balances in less than 30 days. And these are just a few of the strategies that successful businesses use to attract customers without focusing exclusively on price.

There is a common slogan in marketing that states, "There are riches in niches." Simply put, this slogan means you need to determine who your most profitable, enjoyable and easy to attract customer is, and then specialize in getting more of those customers to come into your business and buy. The best way to do this is to create a U.S.P. (Unique Selling Proposition) that compels your most profitable customer to come back into your business again and again. In other words, a U.S.P. is the thing that you're known for.

The first step in developing a U.S.P. is to determine the profile of your most profitable customer. You will want to know things like; how they found your business, where they live, what newspapers and magazines they read etc.

Here's an example of some of the information that you may discover about your prospects and customers:

- Wives initially visited your business without their husbands.
- Recently married
- Had three kids
- Lived within five miles of your business
- Spent between $800 - $1500
- Paid by Visa, MasterCard or Discover

Once you have this information, you can redesign your business to cater to more of the same types of customers that are currently spending money in your business.

However, you can only use this information to your advantage if you take the time to collect it in the first place. Then you can dig deep and find out who your customer is, what's important to them and what they truly want.

CHAPTER 5

Knowing and Having a Calendar Blueprint

There is an timeless saying that goes like this: "Failing to plan means you are planning to fail." That saying is twice as true when it comes to running a business. See, most business owners will not be able to weather this economic storm simply because they don't have the foggiest clue about what promotions or ads they are going to be running in the next week, much less in the next month or year! However, this must change if you are going to survive and thrive in this new economy.

Now, coming up with a twelve month marketing plan may seem like a daunting task, but most of the work is already completed for you. How, you ask? Well, customers are already expecting you to have a special sale or promotion at least once a month, on the major holidays. Therefore, you don't have to recreate the wheel; you can just ride the wave of marketing and advertising messages that are already around that time frame.

While the dates are already set on the calendar, it is still important that you have compelling words and language in your advertisements that reward your customers for buying from you on that specific holiday. Do NOT run a general advertisement that simply says you have stuff on sale. Your ads need to match the holiday theme as closely as possible.

The other benefit you receive from creating a yearly marketing calendar is you will gain a feeling of confidence and reassurance because you are not just sitting on your hands, day-in and day-out, waiting for customers to just walk in and *maybe* buy something from you.

Let's look at a sample twelve-month marketing calendar that you could create around monthly holidays:

- January – New Year's
- February – Valentine's Day
- March – President's Day
- April – April Fool's/Easter
- May – Mother's Day
- June – Father's Day
- July – Fourth of July
- August – (There are no major U.S. Holidays, so do a friends and family sale)
- September – Labor Day
- October – Halloween
- November – Thanksgiving
- December - Christmas

Planning around the months is like planning for weather. You will not dress like you live in Texas if you live in Minnesota. You plan for the weather, if you know it is going to snow tomorrow you get your winter gear ready. Just like if you know it is going to be ninety degrees and humid you know to wear summer clothes.

This same concept goes for you Marketing Blueprint, Market to your prospects and customers when the season and time calls for it. Knowing when to market and what to market is business specific therefore you as the business owner/manager should align your plan with your business goals. Watch what happens to your business after you execute your Marketing Blueprint successfully.

CHAPTER 6

How To Quickly Boost Your Profits By Bringing In The Experts

If your son, daughter or spouse were involved in a car accident and needed specialized attention from a specific type of doctor, would you attempt to perform the surgery yourself in your garage at home? Of course not. It sounds ridiculous to even suggest such a thing, doesn't it? Well, that's how ridiculous it sounds when I hear business owners, who have never even created one single successful advertisement in their twenty years in business, tell me that they refuse to hire marketing consultants.

The sad reality is most business owners know they have major problems with closing ratios, marketing, sales scripts and getting customers into their business. However, they refuse to invest the necessary money to bring in experts to fix their problems.

After speaking with dozens of business owners, I have come to the conclusion that failure to get expert advice is mostly due to business owners having too much pride to ask for help or they have never even considered hiring experts in the first place.

If you really want fast results without wasting money trying out different strategies, then hiring a expert marketing consultant to help you generate more quality buying customers and convert more leads into sales, should be the first thing you do after preparing your mindset for success. Until you hire an expert consultant, you have no idea the numerous benefits your business will gain by having an expert work with you one-on-one.

With an expert marketing consultant in your business, you will no longer feel alone and isolated from other successful business owners. You will no longer feel the doom and dread of having the weight of your business solely on your shoulders. Most importantly, you will have a support system to give you powerful and proven creative ideas to increase your profits.

Now, when I say expert marketing consultant, I'm not referring to some high-priced advertising agency that has no proven track record of increasing sales and profits for small to medium businesses. I am also not talking about the yellow page ad reps, radio ad reps or any other type of advertising representative trying to sell you something. I'm talking about a marketing expert who comes into your office, analyzes your business with a fine-tooth comb and then creates custom marketing and sales improvement strategies for your business that don't cost you a fortune.

PART TWO:

Business Strategies To Generate More Sales and Increase Revenue

CHAPTER 7

Capture Contact Info And Create A List Of Quality Leads

Capturing your leads and prospects contact information when they visit your business, website or call-in, must be the foundation of your business strategies. This simple concept is a powerful and effective strategy being used by many successful businesses all over the world, but for some reason, many business owners allow prospects and leads to waltz in and out of their businesses without even getting their name, email address or phone number.

Have you ever considered how powerful and profitable effective follow up campaigns can be to your business? Most business owners know the truth of this strategy, but have never taken the time to implement it. Once you see how much money you are leaving on the table, you are going to kick yourself in the butt for not doing it sooner.

The other benefit of capturing your prospects contact information is you gain the peace of mind that comes with being able to generate sales at will. You no longer have to sit on the sidelines day after day while your business has little to no customers or clients walking in the door. Now, you can control your monthly profits with precise accuracy by just doing a campaign.

Let's look at the numbers to see just how profitable this strategy is:

Example 1:

- 300 leads into your business per month
- 5% closing ratio = 15 buyers
- $500 average sale
- 100 prospects x 5% closing ratio x $500 average purchase = $7,500 in sales per month.

However, in the example above you never get a chance to sell to the other 95 prospects because you neglected to get their contact information, so that is a ton of missed opportunity. Now, look at the same example as if you captured their contact information and were able to get another five percent to come back and purchase from your business with a future compelling sale promotion.

Example 2:

Now assume that you were able to get an additional 5% of your prospects to return back into your business and purchase using a follow up campaign:

- 300 leads into your business per month
- 10% closing rate (5% initial closing ratio PLUS 5% who buy later from your follow-up campaign = 15 buyers)
- $500 average sale
- 300 prospects x 30 buyers x $500 average purchase = $15,000 per month!

Instead of $7,500 in sales you are now making $15,000 in sales! That is an impressive jump in sales that can be achieved simply by collecting your prospects' contact information and then following up by mail, email or phone. The best part is that all you have to do is get them back into your business and continue closing at the same ratio you already are and you can easily double your sales per month. Now, do you see how powerful and profitable this strategy can be?

However, just like many of the strategies revealed in this book, you must have proven and effective conversion scripts and systems in place to consistently and predictably get these customers back into your business to purchase from you.

Finally, you may be thinking that prospects are not willing to give you their contact information, but that is not true. The key to getting their contact information is to give them a special offer in exchange for them giving you their contact information; most importantly an offer that gets the customer back into your store. For example, you can offer to mail them out special promotions or offer to enter their name in a free prize giveaway. You can even offer to give them a percentage off their next purchase in exchange for their contact information. Many of the biggest and most successful businesses in the world spend thousands of dollars building a list of prospects that may not be ready to buy from them today, because they know it means millions of dollars in profits in the future.

Okay so what's next, how do you bring your business to the next level? Well now that you are aware that you are probably losing money every single day, by not having a proven and powerful phone answering script that's designed to capture your customers contact information.

Let me prove it to you. When someone calls your business asking for directions to your location, what do you give them? Directions, of course. When a customer calls and asks you the price for delivery, what do you give them? Delivery price, of course. Well, do you know if and when that person on the phone is planning on coming into your business? Do you know if they are even planning to come into your business at all? The answer is probably not.

However, what if you offered incoming phone call prospects the option to take advantage of the special sale you are having for today only for 5% - 10% off for first-time buyers, if they come to your business today to make a purchase. Do you think that would give them an incentive to come into your business today? What about offering to put them on a mailing list for the next big promotions or sale that you are having without flooding their inbox? See, your priorities for every incoming phone call you receive from a prospect should be the following:

- Collect their name, phone and email address so you can add them to your follow-up campaign.
- Record the reason why they are calling as well as the products and services they are interested in, so you know what your marketplace wants.
- If you have a product you can sell, offer them the option to purchase by phone, if they already know what they want.
- Get them to commit to coming into your business today by setting an appointment.

Now each business may very due to products or services but if you are truly seeking profitable success with your incoming phone calls, it is also important that you select and train your best staff person to answer your phone. I am fairly confident that you have someone on your staff that sounds nice, pleasant and professional on the phone and truly enjoys talking to customers. This is the type of person you want answering your phones on a daily basis. With a proven script, you will be surprised at how many prospects will give you a chance to earn their business simply because someone spoke nicely to them, captured their contact information and set an appointment.

You also will want to train this staff person to follow-up on outgoing calls to prospects and leads that are in your marketing funnel. Sometimes prospects just need to know that someone cares enough about their needs and wants, to make a little extra effort. This simple little strategy has paid huge rewards for my clients, and it doesn't cost you one extra penny.

CHAPTER 8

Transform Your Customer Receipts Into Marketing Ads & More Sales

When you go to the grocery store, have you ever noticed that your receipts have coupons on them? Okay, the truth is that most men don't notice those types of things, but with women it is a different story. They collect the coupons so they can use them on their next purchase, but in reality those coupons are just receipts with an offer printed on them. Also, have you ever noticed when you go to a fast food restaurant that they offer to enter your name into a monthly drawing for a one thousand dollar prize if you call into a special number and leave your opinion and feedback?

Have you ever taken the time to think about these things from a business owner's point of view? The reason why these companies use these strategies is because these strategies generate more sales and profits. Grocery stores have been using this strategy for many years because their customers are accustomed to saving coupons and purchasing items which are on sale. The reason why businesses collect customer opinions and feedback is because it allows them to keep their pulse on the rapid changes in the marketplace, while also allowing them to see the areas of their business they need to improve or change.

However, most other businesses have yet to catch on to this profitable strategy. In fact, many business owners in other industries that hire me have never even considered the possibility of having a mini-ad, discount or coupon printed on their sales receipts. You can even have your refer-a-friend rewards program ad on the receipt. This transforms a useless piece of paper into a money-generating magnet, just by making a simple change.

You can also put an ad on your receipts highlighting your testimonial or customer feedback phone number. To do this just call your phone service provider and let them know that you want a voicemail only phone number. This extra voicemail phone number may only costs five or ten bucks a month, but the advantage is tremendous. By using this technique, you discover exactly what your customers want and their view of how their experience went. Once you get the testimonial, you can now use that in all your other advertising to prove to prospects that you are the best option in your market place which provides social proof that you are a leader in your industry.

So after the customer refers a friend and the new customer comes in the store you have to sell them on a product or service. With a testimonial on a product they are interested in and business signs that do the selling for you; your staffs' job and your business profit come easier.

Some of the most valuable real estate in your business is your business signage. If you have been in business any amount of time, then you already know that good business signage can be critical in helping customers find your business. However, have you ever thought about using business signage to actually attract prospects to your business?

When I talk about business signage, I am referring to signs on the outside of your business windows, as I assume your building signage is already completed and cannot be changed. Most of the window business signs owners' use usually says generic stuff like, "Sale," "Financing Terms Available," or "Holiday Sale." In this day and time those types of signs are not worth the plastic they're printed on.

If you really want powerful and effective signs on the windows of your location, you must use signs that state your USP and draw customers in. For example, which one do you think is more powerful: "Sale" or "Guaranteed Same Day Delivery On In-Stock Products Or It's FREE!" Compare these two: "We Sell All Major Appliances" or "FREE Delivery With Any Purchase Over $500!"

The key to having business signage which attracts prospects and customers is to focus on the benefits that customers want. If you have no idea what the customers in your marketplace are looking for, then you need to ask every prospect that comes into your business and use that information to create a U.S.P. Unique Selling Proposition that attracts the right type of prospect.

Another place for you to focus on effective business signage that most businesses overlook is inside your business. Just because you got a prospect to walk into your business doesn't mean that your job is done. In your office, store or building, you must have signs that capture the prospects attention and compel them to ask you about it. Here's a quick test you can perform to see if you have good signage in your business: When is the last time a customer was in your business and pointed to a sign and asked you about that product/program/service/offer? If the answer is never or you cannot remember, then chances are that your in-business signage isn't working as effectively as it could be working.

Effective in- business signage can help your staff close a sale, remind customers of why they came into your business or keep a sale closed for you because customers are constantly reminded of your unique U.S.P.

CHAPTER 9

Mail Monthly Newsletters To Prospects and Mail Quarterly Newsletters To Past Customers

Most business owners usually remember to run ads once in a while, but only a select few choose to mail out a quarterly or monthly newsletter to past customers and prospects. This simple little strategy has been responsible for billions of dollars in profits for small business owners who choose to actually use this strategy in their business. Those who do not use this strategy, often wonder why their customers never come back to purchase from them after many hours of building rapport. This is just one of the reasons and it is as simple as keeping your product or brand on the forefront of your customers' mind.

Using monthly or quarterly newsletters can literally mean the difference between struggling to pay your lease or mortgage each month and making a nice little profit on a slow month.

See, the truth is, no matter how much rapport you may have built with a prospect or customer at the time they were in your office or on the phone with you, the minute they walk out the door, anything and everything is fighting for their attention. They have spouses, children, jobs, relatives, vacations, shopping etc. They may have the best motives and intentions when you talk to them, but the longer you wait to follow up with them, the more they forget you.

Have you ever ran into a prospect or past customer at the grocery store or out in your local community who you felt should have really come back to buy from you? When you ask them what ever happened, they tell you they bought it somewhere else? How did that make you feel? Well, why does that happen? Most of the time it happens because salespeople forget to follow up and you don't have a system in place to make sure that prospects never forget you.

You should be mailing out a promotional or educational/informative piece of literature to your prospects at least once a month or every two weeks. If you are not doing this, then you are losing money left and right to your competitors. However, your newsletter or promotional ad should be written to generate sales, not boring and stale. The only way to make sure that your newsletter or monthly marketing piece is good is by learning to be a good copywriter or using proven mail pieces and articles.

When it comes to sending your past customers your newsletter, you should quarterly and should focus on generating referrals and highlighting your rewards program. You should also put a promotion in your newsletter that rewards your past customers for coming in and purchasing additional products and services from you.

CHAPTER 10

Mail Monthly Offers To Your Past Prospects and Leads

Mailing monthly offers to your past prospects and leads must become as natural to you as breathing and eating. In an earlier chapter I presented the reasons why you should collect your prospects contact information, but collecting the contact information and getting sales from your list of prospects are two different things.

With this strategy, you can choose to include the offer in your newsletter like the previous chapter mentioned or you can send the offer separately. However, don't get stuck in procrastination mode debating what would work better, newsletter or separate offer. Just be sure to mail something every month.

Now, when you begin to consistently implement this strategy, you will begin to get a consistent and predictable flow of buying customers in your business. I'm always surprised at business owners who think that they can make a reliable, consistent income based solely on referral business alone. Sure, getting referrals is great, but do you really control that process? No, of course not. However, when you mail your list, you can control the offer you are presenting to your list of prospects and past customers. You can even choose the day that you want your mail piece to go out to them, so in my experience it' is much better when a business owner controls your own success. So, to start you must hire a professional copywriter or personally create a series of sales, promotions and ads that you can use to automatically send out emails, postcards or letters to your prospects. You want them to think of your business when they are ready to make their purchase.

Your monthly mailers to your list of prospects and leads could be newsletters, coupons, informational booklets, emails and more. The only requirement you must meet with whatever you're mailing out is that it must be effective at generating sales and making you money. You are not trying to build a brand, because building a brand doesn't pay the mortgage. Only closing sales and generating profits and depositing money in your bank account pays the mortgage.

CHAPTER 11

Customized Promotions & Sales
For Every Customer

What if you had the power to look into your customers mind and pinpoint the exact products and services they wanted to buy? How much easier would it be to make huge profits in your business? Well, if you have sold to a customer before, then you already have a glimpse into their wants and needs and you probably have never even realized it. This is why identifying your idea customer/prospect is so important.

One of the most under-appreciated strategies that I commonly see business owners neglect to implement into their business is the tracking of customer purchases in order to offer additional pieces. See, if a customer has already purchased pieces of a specific product line or collection, then you know that 99% of the time they will be willing to consider adding similar products and services. This is one area of your business which can catapult your business profits.

In order for you to use this strategy, you must write orders or generate computerized receipts which give every detail about your customer's purchase. For example, you will want to know the collection name, the exact products or services they purchased, their size, color and price discounting etc. The best way to use this information is to use a computer program to generate your receipts and track your customer's purchases.

Once you have specific information about a customer's purchase, every couple of months you can create a promotion or ad to generate sales. However, when you send the ad to your local print shop to print and mail for you, request that they substitute certain portions of the ad with specific information about each customer. For example, if a customer purchased a specific designer name product, you would use that designer name on the front of the ad, with a special coupon for that specific product. This can all be done automatically, so don't pull a brain muscle trying to figure out how to do this on your own. This strategy can be extremely profitable once it's executed properly.

CHAPTER 12

Create A Series Of Informative Workshops, Classes Or Events To Attract Prospects

One of the easiest ways to instantly generate profits and sales is to piggy-back off other successful ideas and strategies. When you ride the coat tails of other successful trends, you eliminate the learning curve and create instant success. Many financial advisors, money managers and even home supply stores like Home Depot and Loews have been using the strategy of hosting workshops, classes and events for their prospects and customers for many years and it's a big lead generator for them. Many of their classes are booked to capacity and customers and prospects love it.

That's why I highly recommend creating your own type of lead generating and credibility-building workshops, classes or events. As long as you are creating relevant content that your prospects find valuable, easy to implement and entertaining, you will find this to be a successful strategy.

So, the first step is deciding how often you want to offer your workshops. My advice is to have a workshop at least once per month. This allows your prospects to develop a relationship with you while also building your credibility in the eyes of your marketplace. Secondly, decide how long you want your workshops to last. The best length for most businesses would range from sixty to ninety minutes. Once you decide that, then you can begin putting together a outline of the type of information that you would want to give away to your prospects in your workshops. You can choose from several various formats for your workshop. Here are some examples:

- Question & Answer
- Interview The Expert
- Do-It-Yourself
- Product Demonstration

Regardless of the format that you choose, just be sure that the content is relevant, useful and fairly fresh to your marketplace.

After you decide the frequency, length and format of your workshops, the next step is deciding the location and delivery method. There are several different formats you can use to do this depending on your business model. Here are some examples:

- Video – Buy a inexpensive video recorder and film yourself doing your workshop. Then, use a service like Youtube.com to post your video to a special page on your website. Remember to advertise your online video workshop in your regular marketing efforts.

- In-office/Store/Warehouse/Factory Presentations – This is when you have the prospects come to your business location to listen and watch your informative presentation.

- Teleseminars – With this strategy you get a teleconference phone number and have prospects call in on a certain day and time.

- Audio CD – You can record your workshop using software on your computer and then burn copies to a disc. Then, mail them out to your list of prospects.

- Webinars – You can use a service that records your computer screen while you are providing information using a PowerPoint slide presentation.

It's important to remember that this strategy can only be effective if you advertise them aggressively and if your content is relevant to your marketplace. The other good thing about this strategy is that you can really attract the attention of the local media by submitting regularly scheduled press releases and doing email campaigns and feature spots in your monthly and quarterly newsletters for your workshop, class or event. All in all, you can really generate some massive publicity and quality leads by implementing this strategy.

CHAPTER 13

How To Transform Your Customers Into Walking Billboards For Your Business

Whenever someone makes a new purchase, one of the first things they do is brag to their family, friends and neighbors. Your goal in using this strategy is to tap into that excitement and leverage it to create new customers. I like to call this strategy the radius marketing strategy. By using the radius marketing strategy, you can capture that excitement and gain access to new customers. Secondly, most people tend to have friends with similar interests who live in the same neighborhoods. So, when you have a customer who comes into your business and makes a purchase, chances are that their neighborhood is filled with other prospects that would also be able to afford and appreciate your products or services.

In order to use this strategy, you simply take the address of a recent customer and draw an imaginary circle around their house which represents an actual distance of five blocks to ten blocks. Once you have your circle drawn, then you mail out a campaign to those prospects inside of your circle, because those are the neighbors of your current customer. The theme of the campaign is focused around teasing your prospects by revealing that someone in their neighborhood bought from you, so they should as well. You will also offer them a special neighborhood discount because they live in the same area as a current customer. You can map out the addresses close to your current customer and mail them automatically online at the website of the United States Postal Service.

Let's examine a campaign:

- Customer purchases from you, so you go online and purchase a list of addresses of their neighbors.

- Write, create or purchase a series of three to seven mailers consisting of postcards, letters and discount coupons.

- Provide information on your mailers that direct the prospects to a special website specifically designed for neighbors of current customers to capture their email address and offer an incentive to get prospects to set an appointment to visit your business.

- Use a professional printer or online service to schedule your series of mailers to go out automatically to the neighbors of your most recent customers.

CHAPTER 14

Dialing For Dollars:
Using Telemarketing To
Grow Your Business

I n a previous chapter I revealed several ways that you or your staff can increase your sales, appointments and overall sale opportunities by changing the way you answer your business phone. In this chapter, I will discuss the tried and true method of generating prospects and customers using telemarketing. In recent years, telemarketing has gotten a bad reputation because of a few bad companies misusing the technique; however, it is still a very effective marketing strategy when used properly.

There are three important parts to effectively using telemarketing to generate business. The first important key to your success with telemarketing is your list of prospects that you are calling. Your success using this strategy is directly determined by your ability to contact the right type of prospect in the first place. The easiest way to do this is to use your current customer receipts and surveys to discover all of the information about your best customers. Then you can use that information to compile a customer profile. After you have created a customer profile, then it is time to create your list. This can be done by calling a company like www.infousa.com or www.usadata.com and asking them to compile a list of prospects who match the same criteria as your ideal customer profile.

Once you have a list of prospects to call, then your next step is to create an effective phone script. However, in order to create an effective phone script, you have to determine what the goal of your sales call will be. You can choose to write a phone script that sells your product over the phone or you can use the phone script to set appointments for prospect's to come into your business. After you determine the goal of your phone call, then you need to record or write down the transcript of a face-to-face presentation that you or your sales staff has recently conducted. This will allow you to use a proven sales script when you are on the phone with prospects.

The last step in an effective telemarketing campaign is your ability and willingness to follow up with your prospects on a regular basis. When it comes to telemarketing, you must be willing to call weekly, monthly or even daily in some cases in order to have a chance to earn their business.

Following these three key ingredients will give your telemarketing campaign a great chance for success. Without using the key ingredients I listed for you, your telemarketing campaign will most likely be doomed to fail before you even begin. If done properly, telemarketing could be another tool that you have in your arsenal that can help drive prospects into your business.

CHAPTER 15

The Holy Grail Of Marketing: Generating Referrals

While every business owner loves to get referrals, very few have a system in place to consistently generate those referrals. As you probably already know, referrals close at higher rate than most other types of leads, so if you want to take your business to the next level, you should definitely create a system that generates referrals.

In this chapter, I will give you a referral generation plan that will be easy, simple and powerful. However, you should know that there are several key components to creating an effective referral campaign. The first step in creating a powerful referral campaign is to have a product or service that is worth referring. Your product and service must be memorable and perform exactly as it is supposed to, in order for your customers to refer their friends and family to your business. If you have a crappy product that doesn't hold up over time or if you have a service that causes more problems than it solves, then it will be very difficult for the few customers you get to refer others to you.

The second step in creating a referral system is to build your request for referrals into your closing process. However, I am not saying that you should ask for referrals before you close the sale. You should ask for referrals after a customer had decided to buy, but before they leave your business. So, for example, if you are an accountant and you have a client in front of you while you are doing their taxes, then that moment is the perfect time to ask them if they know of anyone who also wants to get their taxes done. If they say yes, you then ask for permission to contact that referral and use the referring person's name.

The last and final component to a successful referral campaign is to find a way to easily and automatically contact your customers and remind them to send you referrals. The best way that I've discovered to accomplish this is by inserting your customers into a monthly or quarterly mailing campaign that is designed to generate referrals. This can be a series of postcards, letters or phone calls that reminds them that you build your business by getting referrals from past customers. Just make sure that whatever method you choose, be sure to do it consistently with all your customers.

CHAPTER 16

The Powerful Profit Potential Of Packaging Your Products And Services

Most businesses in the retail industry have long profited from this strategy, but most service providers neglect to use this strategy to its fullest potential. Packaging your products and services into bundles allows you to charge higher prices and creating the perception in the marketplace that you are a premium product or service provider. The packaging strategy allows you to promote and advertise several other products while initially getting customers to come into your business to purchase other products or services. This dramatically reduces your marketing costs because you are essentially piggy-backing on your current advertising efforts.

For example, if you own a tree-cutting business, then you can offer to cut down one tree for $399 or you can have a package that includes chopping down up to five trees for $999. This package would represent $1,000 in savings for your customers, but it would also allow you to make more profit on every transaction. You could even have a premium package that includes cutting down one tree and landscaping maintenance for one month for $599. See, in this case, you are already in front of the customer for one service, so why not offer them a valuable package that would entice them to purchase more from you.

The one thing that I would caution you to watch out for with this strategy, is the temptation to lower your prices to the point where you are making peanuts for profits and developing a reputation for being the cheapest company in your industry. Being the cheapest is not always the best feature for a business. Even in the most competitive marketplaces you can package your products and services in a way that will allow you to charge a premium price. So, take the time today to sit down and come up with several different ways you can package your products and services.

CHAPTER 17

Up-sell, Cross-sell and Down-sell

When you get a prospect who says they are ready to purchase do you or your staff hurriedly write up the order and process the payment because you are afraid they will change their mind? How many times have you had someone take the time to visit your business, sit through a sales presentation, only to say they want to go and think about it. Well, these are two cases in which you have an alternative option that could result in bigger profits.

If you are like most business owners I consult with, then you probably just process the payment when a customer says they want to buy and let a customer walk when they say they want to go home and think about it. However, I guarantee you that if you are doing those two things, then you are missing out on a ton of cash.

The key to turning the regular sale into a spectacular sale is to have an option for the customer to instantly get more/bigger/better at a great value because they are buying right now. For example, if you are a plumber and you get a call to repair a leaky pipe in a customer's kitchen, then you can go out and just fix the pipe and make your normal fee for fixing a pipe. However, you can also choose to bring out your high end pipes, fittings, faucets and hoses. When you arrive at the customer's home, walk them through a presentation that offers them an optional package that includes all the latest and greatest parts and products. This is called an up-sell because you are selling the customer a package that increases the size of that order. When you offer the customer the option to also get complimentary products and services that accompany the pipe fixing service you offer, that is considered a cross sell. There have been companies who have increased the average amount of the order by 50% or more, just by having an up-sell and a cross-sell.

Now, the down-sell is when you have met with a client or prospect and they chosen not to buy a specific product or service. In this case, you can offer a scaled down version of the product or service for a cheaper price. This works really well when you attract customers to your business based on a package of products or services and as they raise objections, you can begin to strip the package apart and offer single items or services for a reduced price.

These strategies have been proven to work for thousands of companies who have chose to implement these profit building systems. Now, it's time for you to harness the power of these strategies too.

CHAPTER 18

Partnering With Other Businesses That Sell Complimentary Products And Services

Partnering with other businesses to promote your business is a joint venture strategy that few business owners ever consider. It's probably because this joint venture strategy will require you to be really confident and comfortable in your own business. Otherwise, it would seem like you are risking losing your customers to another business, but that is not true. The key to this strategy is partnering with companies that don't sell the same types of products or services that you sell. Now, just to be clear about this strategy; you will not be exchanging the addresses of your customers with other businesses, you will be creating a in-business coupon or referral program that other businesses will give out to their customers or prospects.

When you partner with other businesses who sell complementary products and services to the same target market that you do, it allows you to gain access to your joint venture partner's customers who may be in the market for products or services you sell. For example, if you are an accountant who finds that working with business owners is your most profitable niche, then you should look to partner with money managers, consultants and marketing firms because they also work with business owners. Now, when I say partner with these other businesses, what I mean is to work out a mutually beneficial relationship with them. For example, you could host an informative workshop together and both of you send out a mailer to your list of past customers and both of you share the costs of the mailer and event location.

If you are having a problem coming up with some potential joint venture partners, here are a few questions to get the ball rolling:

- What other business or services sell related services to your customers?
- What other related products or services do your customers need that you don't have the ability to sell them?
- What friends or family members do you know that own a business?
- What are some local businesses that you would really like to help succeed.

CHAPTER 19

Profitable Partnerships:
Partner With Your Customers

Out of all the joint venture strategies I know, the most important joint venture strategy is the one that includes your customers. Many companies call this a referral strategy, but I think of it as a referral strategy and a joint venture strategy. See, if you are rewarding your customer with the right incentives, they will work their butts off for your success.

The best joint venture strategy I've seen with customers involved is the referral bucks program. With this program you reward your past customers with business bucks for referring someone who purchases over a certain amount in your business and mentions your customer's name as the referring party. If you structure your program this way, then your customers will begin to pre-qualify the friends and people that they refer to you.

This is a powerful strategy, but only if you are providing a quality product and good service. It's also powerful because you can train your customers to buy from you in certain dollar amounts to qualify for certain rewards. This allows you to influence your average purchase amount, which then allows you to increase your profit margins.

It always amazes me that more businesses don't use this strategy. It really is a great program when applied correctly. If you want to take it up a notch then send each one of your customers ten or twenty referral cards which look like business cards, but it has a blank spot for them to write their name and phone number on it. You may also want to include a special discount coupon on the card, so that their referral would be sure to give the referring customers' name when visiting your business. This way you train your customers to always be on the lookout for referrals, because it actually pays for them to refer people to you. You may also want to max your referral bucks at a specific amount that can be redeemed for each purchase once your program gets rolling along.

PART THREE:

Online & Internet Strategies That Generate Tons Of Prospects And Customers

CHAPTER 20

Build A Website That Actually Generates Sale

Imagine waking up at 7 am in the morning and already having sold five thousand dollars worth of your products through your website. Imagine checking your email after breakfast and finding that you have three appointments that were booked during the night! That's the feeling you can experience on a daily basis once you create an effective website for your business. Now, when I say effective website, I am NOT talking about just having a "pretty brochure" website for your friends and family members to compliment you on. I'm talking about a website that generates leads and automatically transforms visitors into buying customers.

A website that actually generates money may seem like a far-fetched idea for most business owners, but it doesn't have to be a fantasy for you. However, you must be willing to make a few simple changes. For most business owners, therein lies the problem. See, chances are that you don't have the foggiest idea about what it takes to turn your basic website into a money maker. So, in this chapter I will give you some direction on the steps you must take in order to transform your website expense into a stream of revenue.

The first component of a successful website is making sure that your website looks professional and clearly shows your products, services, prices, specs and contact phone number and directions to your business. There is nothing more frustrating than having to search all over a website to find a phone number or office address. If you have a reputable business, then you should post as much information on your website about your products and services as possible.

Secondly, your website must have a opt-in form to capture your prospects email address. You have probably seen this email opt-in form on other websites that you frequent. An opt-in form is a place on your website that asks a website visitor for their email address in exchange for something like a free report, discount coupon or newsletter subscription. However, you must offer highly desirable "lead bait" in exchange for a prospect's email address. When it comes to lead bait, it's important that your prospects view your offer as valuable and are willing to give you their email address, your lead bait can be just about anything.

Third, your website must have a method to connect with website visitors in a personal way. You can use video, audio or a simple headshot photo on the homepage which gives the website visitor a personalized greeting from you. The video can be recorded with a simple digital camera and then uploaded to YouTube.com. Once it's on YouTube, you can then put the video on your website. If you already have a website, then you can get your web designer and tech guy to make all of these specific changes.

The fourth change should be making sure you have emails pre-programmed into your website, which are automatically sent out to prospects who signed up to receive your bait. By pre-programming your emails, it appears as if you are following up with every prospect personally. This will give you the ability to follow up with your leads automatically for as long as you want.

These are just a few of the major changes which should be made to your website in order to convert prospects into customers. There are many more changes, but the one principle you need to remember is this: hire an experienced marketer to design your website to sell. Don't make the mistake of allowing a graphic designer or tech guy design your website without the input and guidance of an experienced marketer. Otherwise, you will have a beautiful website that never makes you a dime.

CHAPTER 21

Increasing Sales With
Pay Per Click

Most business owners realize the benefits of website marketing, but many owners do little to nothing to get their website in front of prospective customers on a consistent basis. See, having a website built for your business and getting your website up and running online is only the first step. However, your website won't make you one measly sale, if you are not able to get it in front of prospective customers who are willing, ready and able to spend money to purchase your products or services.

There are dozens of strategies to generate leads and prospects online, but in the next several chapters, I will cover the most profitable and easy to set up strategies that I have come across in my years of internet marketing.

One of the cheapest and quickest strategies to get up and running is the pay per click strategy. If you haven't heard of pay per click before, then let me give you a brief overview.

When you visit a search engine website like Google.com and type in a word or phrase and click enter, you will see a webpage which shows the results of the search you entered. On the very top of the page you will see two or three search results that will be highlighted in a shaded box that has a different color than the rest of the page. On the far right of the webpage you will also notice a row of eight to ten ads. The ads at the top and right of the search results page are ads placed there by companies who pay anywhere from five cents to five dollars to show up as an advertiser for a specific word. However, they only pay the fee if a potential customer clicks on the ad. There is also a bidding component to pay per click, which means that many advertisers are bidding a certain amount to be near the top of the list of advertisers on the search results webpage.

Using pay per click is such a powerful strategy that many million dollar companies have been built on the back of this one strategy. However, there are several key components to this strategy which must be in place to turn it into a money maker for your business.

The keys to success when using pay per click are:

- Bid in amounts until you get really good at it.

- Write a compelling ad which attracts the right type of prospective customer.

- Have a special website designed specifically for your pay per click campaign. Your normal website will not make you one penny in most cases if you just plug it into your pay per click campaign.

- Hire an expert pay per click manager if you can't get the hang of it.

CHAPTER 22

Writing and Submitting Informative & Educational Articles Online

When customers begin shopping for a new product or service, they often start by finding as much information as possible about vendors, quality and local businesses. The number one goal of most customers is to find products or services with decent quality in a price range that they can afford. The only way to locate these products and vendors is to do the research about products and services online before purchasing.

In order to make a good impression on the prospect that is doing their research and homework, you have to make sure that you are putting your business information in a place where consumers will easily find it. There is no better way to do this than by writing informative and educational articles and having them posted on websites where your target prospects are likely to be searching.

Writing and submitting articles to online directories allows you to really control the flow of information about your products and services in your local market. I have had tremendous success using short articles containing about four to five hundred words to generate leads and prospects. You don't have to be the next Tom Clancy or Stephen King in order to get prospects to read your articles. All you have to do is write a short couple of paragraphs about a particular collection, promotion or sale that you currently are advertising.

The subject of the articles should be educational but also slightly entertaining. The last thing you want to be is boring and sounding like you are writing a users manual. Consumers want to know that your products, services and business will provide a good quality product, but consumers also like to work with businesses that are fun, exciting and helpful.

If you are a pretty good writer, you can write your own articles to promote your business, however, I strongly suggest hiring a freelance writer to submit one or two articles per week on your behalf to the top ten or twenty online directories.

Writing and submitting articles to online directories will help to boost your rankings in popular search engines like Google.com and Yahoo.com. These search engines will give your website higher priority when a prospect types in a keyword and will give you a better chance to you to show up as one of the first ten choices in your target market.

CHAPTER 23

Partnering Online With Other Websites

I f having a website that actually generates sales is a rare thing for a small to medium business, then partnering with other websites to swap or purchase advertising space must seem next to impossible. However, once you have a website that attracts your target customer, then partnering with other websites to help each other generate customers is not that far of a reach. This is another strategy which seems intimidating on the surface level, but once you get started, it's actually pretty simple.

Obviously this strategy requires that you have a website; however, there is another step you must complete before implementing this strategy. The first step is having a graphic designer create several various size web banners for you to market your business on other websites. The next step is making sure that you can actually post ads on your website or have your webmaster or tech guy post them online. Once this step is done, you can them move on to implementing the strategy.

The easiest way to implement this strategy is to start by researching the local businesses that you currently use on a ongoing basis. The first step you should do is visit online search engine www.google.com and enter their business name and find out if they even have a website. If they have a website that looks decent then visit their business just like normal and speak to the owner or the person in charge of marketing and introduce yourself. If you are not recognized by anyone, then let them know that you are a regular customer.

Once you have introduced yourself, let them know that you have a website and you would like to do an ad swap with them. Let them know that you will promote their business for free on your website, but you would like free advertising on their website as well. This should be enough of a hook for a semi-intelligent business owner to move forward with the partnership. However, if they don't bite on this, then just move on to the next local business that you frequent and make the same offer.

There are two key notes to mention when using this strategy. The first key is make sure you have tracking software installed on your website, so you will know exactly which advertising partner each prospect is coming from. Secondly, make sure the prospect is redirected to a specific webpage that is optimized to sell to these type of customers. Your website manager should know how to do both of these fairly easily.

CHAPTER 24

Make Sure Prospects Find You Online And Not Your Competitors

Most of the time, having a beautiful website that highlights your products, services, office and staff is a wonderful and necessary marketing tool. However, you will never make a single penny from your website if prospective customers cannot find your website online.

Every business owners I consult with knows that he needs a website, but virtually none know how to guarantee that their prospective customers find their website before finding their competitor's website. So in this chapter I will reveal how you can practically guarantee that your prospects find your website before your competitor's.

Having a general idea about how search engines work is the first step in making sure prospects can find your website online. Search engines are websites like Google.com, Yahoo.com and Bing.com. These websites compile tons of data and information and make sifting through it manageable by organizing it by order of importance to the "keyword" you typed into your browser. For example, if you type in "pizza restaurants in Milford, CT" into your search engine browser, then you will get the most relevant pizza restaurants in Milford, CT that your search engine feels ranks most closely to the phrase or keyword term you typed in. That's why you want your website and the pages on your website to match as closely to the relevant terms for your target market as possible.

Understanding how prospects search online is the second thing you must understand in order to ensure that prospects find your website. For example, if a customer is looking for a plumber who specializes in working with gold plated piping, then you need to have a webpage on your website that is especially designed for those type of customers. The simplest way to think of this concept is by focusing on "buyer keywords."

Buyer keywords are words that prospects type into their search engine browser to find places to buy the product or service they are looking for. For example, if you were a furniture store owner, who do you think is a more serious prospect: the customer who types in "sofa bed sales for memorial weekend," or the customer who types in "sofa bed"? So, if you had to choose between designing a webpage on your website for generic sofa beds or designing a specific webpage for sofa bed sales for memorial weekend, which one should you choose?

CHAPTER 25

Advertise Your Website URL On Everything In Your Business

Promoting the heck out of your website is one very effective but underrated online strategy that can have a dramatic impact on your bottom line. As I already established in early chapters, just having a website and putting it online is not enough to get money in your bank account. Many business owners I consult with are under the false impression that having a website is the savior of their business. This couldn't be further from the truth.

In today's technologically advanced culture, having a website is simply mandatory. In fact, you are viewed as a dinosaur if you do not have website. From a customer's perspective, having a website is not seen as a huge advantage. From a customer's perspective every business should have a website.

It's best to view your website as a separate tool that you could use to generate sales, instead of viewing it as the answer to all your sales woes. After all, it's not the website that sets you apart; it is about your USP and your ability to consistently attract customers to your website. Once you get prospects to your website, your next job is to actually write words and use images on your website that compel your customer to open their wallet, take out their credit card and purchase from you.

Your website address should be advertised on your business cards, sales receipts, business windows, business signage, and product information spec sheets and anywhere else you can think of. This strategy works even better if you have a memorable website address. For example, if you were a mortgage broker, then consider the following website address: www.guaranteedlowestinterestrate.com. That would at least catch your attention if you saw it and you were in the market for a loan. The important key is to remember that your website does nothing for you unless you get visitors to your website and then are able to convert them into buyers.

CHAPTER 26

The Power Of Craigslist.com

In the last decade, customers purchasing products online have accounted for tens of billions of dollars in sales. However, millions of those dollars have changed hands as a direct result of having been seen on a popular website Craigslist.com. In fact, every month millions of Americans shop online at the popular free website called Craigslist.com. One of my most popular strategies for a business that sells a product consists of advertising your entry level, slightly damaged or discontinued products online for reduced prices on Craigslist. This would allow you generate profits from products that traditionally just sits in your warehouse for months or years and collects dust.

The best part about Craigslist.com is the fact that it's free to advertise unlimited products on the website. The biggest obstacle you will face when advertising on Craigslist.com is the uploading of images and writing descriptions about the products you are selling. However, you can have one of your staff members specialize in posting your listings on the website on a daily basis, so you don't personally have to do the work.

You may also want to consider advertising on other online classified ad websites like www.backpage.com or www.kiji.com. These website work much like Craigslist.com, but they do not get the volume of visitors and prospects. Using these free classified ad websites is a much quicker and profitable way to sell your entry level merchandise and slightly used products, than waiting around for the product to become obsolete. You may also want to consider working your new and regular merchandise into your Craigslist.com marketing strategy.

CHAPTER 27

The Proven Power Of
Email Marketing

Over the past several years, having a website has become the standard expectation of successful s business. Most business owners have either purchased a website or have a simple webpage that directs visitors to their business. However, less than one percent of small to medium businesses utilize effective email marketing campaigns to give customers incentives to purchase from their businesses after their initial visit to the website or showroom. Neglecting to implement an effective email marketing campaign is the same as leaving thousands of dollars lying around on the ground each month.

Since I've began helping business owners increase their sales and profits, I have discovered the reason why so many business owners miss out on the easy profits from their website. The number one reason for missing out on the easy profits is because most business owners do not actually get their prospects' or customers' email address. If you never have the email address then you cannot possibly use it to market to your prospects and past customers.

When I say email marketing, I'm not just talking about collecting email addresses of customers who have emailed you with questions, because most times that doesn't really happen. In order to have an effective email marketing campaign, you must have enticing bait that customers will get in exchange for giving you their email address. For example, if you were an accountant, your "email bait" could be a coupon, rewards program or a simple informative report titled, "7 Insider Strategies to Hiring An Accountant" or a similar title. In order to capture the email address you can use a service that I recommend by visiting www.aweber.com

Once you have the email address you can then send out emails about sales, promotions or informative. However, you cannot just send out emails begging prospects or customers to buy. Your emails must be fun, educational and timely. Therefore, unless you are a professional writer and marketer, you will want to hire a professional marketer to write your emails and suggest the best frequency to send them out.

CHAPTER 28

Creating A Weekly Or Monthly
Online Newsletter

If you truly want to explode your profits and sales in your business, then get out of the salesman mentality and get into the relationship building mentality. When you began to see your prospects and customers as people who can become your friends and extended family, you will treat them differently. Many times over the years I have seen customers become irate and cancel orders simply because the salesperson treated them with a cold detached manner, instead of talking to them as a friend. Building relationships with your customers has to be your number one priority if you want to create customers for life.

One of the ways in which you can build a relationship with your prospects and customers is by sending out fun, education and entertaining newsletters once per eek/month/quarter. At a minimum you should send out the newsletters once a quarter to your past customers and once a month to your prospects that you've collected email addresses from.

It is very important that the content of your newsletter be natural and not too well polished. The reality is, the more down to earth and simple your newsletter is, the more customers will be able to relate to you through your newsletter. In fact, the last thing you want to do is create a slick looking newsletter that uses words, phrases and pictures that are nothing like what you would actually say or do. Remember, this is about building a relationship with you and your business. It's not about putting out the most professional newsletter on the planet.

The content of your newsletter should include pictures of you and your staff. You should also include pictures of your customers having fun or purchasing in your business. It is also a good idea to include a contest or sweepstakes which rewards customers for reading the newsletter and answering hidden questions in the newsletter. You also want the newsletter to be laid back and not just industry jargon and talk. Most of your customers don't know industry jargon and don't care about it, but they do care about their pets, gardening and recipes. As silly as it sounds, you want your newsletter to be written for the normal guy and gal. Of course, you want to put a section promoting your products and services too, but that should be a small percentage of your newsletter.

PART FOUR:

Publicity Strategies That Generate Huge Profits At Little To No Cost

CHAPTER 29

Writing Articles For Magazines and Newspapers

The perfect marketing plan should include both paid advertising strategies and free publicity strategies. In fact, free publicity marketing strategies are much more effective in promoting your business than 99% of paid marketing strategies. However, you need both strategies in order to provide a constant stream of growth and profits.

One of the best methods you can use to generate tons of free publicity for your business without coming across as a pushy salesperson, is writing articles for newspapers or magazines. This strategy can pay huge dividends especially when you become as the "go-to" expert for a publication that your target market reads on a regular basis.

Writing articles for magazines and newspapers not only gets you recognition from your target market, but this strategy also helps you become a magnet for other free publicity opportunities. It is a great feeling to have prospects visit your business and buy from you because you are the expert in your niche. That feeling is a lot different than having people shop your prices all over town, visit your business and receive excellent service from you, but then go and buy from somewhere else because the other business was ten cents cheaper. The best way to avoid being shopped to death is to become the obvious go-to expert for your niche.

The reason why writing articles for magazines and newspapers works so well is because we are all taught from a young age to believe what the newspapers tell us. The majority of people in our culture believe news stories as if they are the gospel. When you become part of the experts that the newspapers and magazines rely on for their information, then you become known as the expert. Your customers will begin to believe everything you tell them as factual and truthful instead of questioning your every little move and decision.

The best way to get your articles included in a newspaper or magazine is to write three to twelve articles and have them professionally edited. You can then contact your local newspaper or target magazines and offer to be a guest writer or offer your articles for inclusion in their publication.

CHAPTER 30

Using Press Releases To Quickly Generate Sales

Writing press releases is the quickest and easiest way to get local and national media outlets to notice and promote your business. Unfortunately, most business owners only think about using a press release with a grand opening. However, you should be sending out a press release at least once or twice a month, but only if you have a marketing plan that includes professionally prepared press releases which are informative, educational and entertaining.

By this point, you may be asking yourself why local and nation media would be interested in your business. Well, the truth of the matter is that radio, newspaper and television stations all need news stories on a regular basis. Media outlets must have enough news to fill their air time and pages of their newspapers. Without stories to talk about newspapers, magazines and news reports become very boring and mundane.

If you implement a regular press release campaign in your business, you will begin to get offers to be in your local media. Over time you will become a local celebrity in your target market, and that will allow you to attract prospects to your business because they want to be associated with a celebrity who is successful.

Just like with many of the other strategies, your press release strategy can only work effectively if hire a marketing-minded writer or become a good marketing-minded writer who knows how to write in a way that compels prospects to actually take the necessary action and visit your business. Do not make the mistake of thinking that any press release will be good enough. You must either learn the skill of copywriting or hire a professional copywriter to create your compelling press releases.

CHAPTER 31

Sponsor Local Charity Events

S ponsoring local charity events is another great strategy to build up goodwill towards your business while getting your message across to your target market. Sponsoring local charity events is not a new strategy, but it hasn't really been embraced on a larger scale by many small to medium businesses. However, now that you know about this highly effective strategy, you can reap the rewards of implementing it into your business.

The key to profiting from sponsorship of local charity events is to hone in on your target market and discover what charity events they will be most interested in attending. This requires you to gather information from your target market, which you cannot do unless you ask your customers for their input on your website or in your business.

Once you gather information from your past and current customers, then you can begin to look for sponsorship opportunities that match your target market. There are thousands of sponsorship opportunities right in your local area. The fastest way to find a sponsorship opportunity is to contact non-profit organizations which match your target markets interests.

It is important for you to know that sponsorship opportunities will require an investment from your business ranging from a few hundred dollars to several thousand dollars. Most sponsorship opportunities will have various levels, so don't worry about being locked into a huge expensive contract.

When deciding on a specific non-profit organization or cause to champion, make sure that your business or businesses receive maximum coverage on the specific organizations' website and marketing material. Remember that the goal of your sponsorship opportunities is to bring exposure to your businesses. However, you can choose a charity event that has significance to you, but just make sure that it serves dual purposes, otherwise it will make you feel really good, but won't generate the desired amount of free publicity for your business.

CHAPTER 32

Testimonials

Testimonials are an excellent way to build consumer confidence in your products or services. Visitors to your site witness actual clients and their level of satisfaction with your company. They see how your products are put to use and get ideas as to how they can use them also. You can add video testimonials for maximum impact, as they appeal to everyone — even those who typically don't take time to read websites and create a type of social proof that helps your personal branding. Alternatively you can post a testimonial in text form with accompanying pictures of the client and even the client using your company's services or products. You can also use simple audio clips for testimonials.

Some tips for the use of testimonials:

- Get testimonials from both genders
- If your product or service is used in a variety of different ways or industries, get testimonials from various areas
- Put some diversity of age and ethnicity in your testimonials
- Feel free to use just a portion of a testimonial if it is too lengthy
- Ask customers for testimonials that you can use

New customers feel more confident about their decision to

purchase from you if you have testimonials on your site. They get the impression that they are a part of a group and that they are not just another sale.

In every testimonial, you must include:

- Customer's name and title
- City and state
- Credentials

Encourage them to talk about the way your business helped to solve their problem. Always get permission from the person to use the testimonial and information in it before publishing it. Keep a copy of the permission for reference.

PART FIVE:

High-Powered
Advanced Marketing Strategies

CHAPTER 33

Online Reputation Management

Your reputation is important. Unflattering news, pictures, negative reviews, blog posts, and comments about your person, your business, brand, products and services can be posted and spread instantaneously throughout the online world fast damaging your status and affect your sales and bottom line. You cannot afford not to do ORM! Your online reputation is your image on the Internet. Online reputation management (ORM) is about improving or restoring your name or your brand's good standing. This is by countering, weakening or eliminating the negative material found in the Internet defeating it with more positive material to improving your credibility and customers' trust in you.

Do you Google yourself or your company and not like what you see?

- **44%** of adults online have searched for information about someone whose services or advice they seek in a professional capacity, like a doctor, lawyer or plumber
- **50%** of ALL Internet users over the age of 18 have left a review online
- **78%** of Internet users conduct product research online; they believe reviews are the most credible form of advertising
- **80%** of people surveyed had changed a purchase decision due to a bad review they saw online

More and more companies are buckling up for negative social media buzz, which can threaten a brand's online reputation. You need to be prepared as well. Start with proper ORM for your business today.

CHAPTER 34

Be A Radio Show Guest
On Local Stations

An effective strategy which attracts customers by the carloads is to become a local celebrity. One of the fastest ways to become well known in a marketplace is to be everywhere your target market hangs out or shops. One of the ways to build your celebrity status is to become a regular guest on the local radio circuit. Very few business owners have ever considered being a radio guest as a way to connect with their prospects and customers while growing their business.

The reason why being a radio show guest is so effective is because radio show hosts have already taken the time to build relationships with their listeners and you can piggyback off of their success. The truth of the matter is that every radio station needs guests to fill their airtime for their audience.

The first step in this process is to figure out the radio programs that your prospects listen to on a regular basis. You can accomplish this by asking your customers and prospects on a survey form on your website or in your business. You can reward them for providing the information by giving them a coupon for a discount.

Once you have that information, you should begin to listen to those specific radio stations for at least a week or more. Listening to the station will provide you with the general flow and outline of the best programming on that station. After you get a good feel for a station, you can then begin to come up with an interesting angle or story hook to get their attention.

When you have your story angle or hook, you can then hire a writer to write a press release around your idea. You can hire a pretty good writer from websites like www.cragislist.com or www.getafreelancer.com. The writer should also be able to send your press releases to your target radio shows at least once or twice each month for a monthly retainer fee. Your press release will also give the radio station your contact information and story idea. If the radio station chooses your story idea they will contact you for more information on your story idea. Of course, your ultimate goal is to be invited to be a guest for one of their shows.

Being a radio show guest does require some skills which you will have to develop in order to be a good guest. For example, you must be entertaining, educational and quick on your feet. It's very much like working with a customer in your office or business, except that you will be speaking into microphone. There are several programs online which instruct you on how to be a radio show guest, so you may want to invest in one of those programs before implementing this strategy into your business.

CHAPTER 35

Guest Blog On a Popular Local Blog/Website

Being a guest blogger on other local blogs and websites is one of the more advanced and effective online strategies. This is one step away from being a true joint venture strategy, but it is equally as effective when done properly. In fairness, this strategy does require that you be a decent writer and have the ability to "write on demand". If your writing skills are not up to par, you can always hire a writer to write short articles for you and then post those articles on other blogs.

The huge benefit of this strategy is your implied positioning as the go-to expert to your target market, simply because you are the author of a informative and educational blog posting. However, in order to accomplish this goal, you must partner with blogs and websites which cater to your target market.

The best way to discover who your target market really is, is to review your previous customer receipts or order forms and compile the information into a spreadsheet or computer document. Once you have the information into a easily understandable format, you can then analyze the data to see specific patterns and trends.

Your next step is to find customers, friends or family members who match the same target demographic as your past customers. Ask them for recommendations of websites and blogs which they frequently visit. You may get lucky and be able to be a featured guest blogger on one of the websites they mention or you may have to find similar websites in your local target market. In either case, your business will greatly benefit from you being viewed as a source of credible information about your products and services.

Once you find websites or blogs that match your target market, there are several ways to contact the blog authors and owners. The first method is a little more stealthy, but basically you just post comments on their blog for a couple of weeks and then email them to let them know that you have written a couple of articles which would make a very good blog posting for a specific niche. It's important that you don't come across as a salesperson for your business or a specific product, but as a author you is willing to provide some informative blog postings for their blog audience.

The second way to contact blog authors and owners is to email them and ask directly if you could be a guest blogger. You will have to email them a copy of your articles that you have written or have paid to have written for you. Once they see that you are serious about giving them good information to post on their blogs, you will definitely have a better chance of becoming a regular guest blogger.

CHAPTER 36

Start Your Own Blog

Most business owners are content to simply have a nice website, but super-successful small to medium businesses know that they may need something more for their online strategies to be successful. That's why having a blog becomes more of a necessity.

A blog is a website that allows you to add text, video or pictures instantly without needing to know computer coding or hiring tech guys to reprogram your website. Websites like Wordpress.com and Blogger.com will give you a free blog and will walk you through the setup process.

One of the great features of having a blog is your ability to post content online, therefore communicating with your target market without expensive advertising or marketing costs. Blogs also have a feature which allows your visitors to post comments and text, videos or pictures of their own. This allows you to build a relationship of communication with your target prospects. Of course, this comes with some risk. If you have a prospect or customer who is not happy with your company, product or service, then your blog may serve as a most convenient place for them to voice all of their disapproval.

However, the best benefit of having a blog is the ability to plug into other popular "social media" websites which are heavily visited by internet users in every target market in the world. Social media websites are websites where the visitors and users have the ability to interact with each other and create online groups or communities of individuals of similar interests.

The success of most strategies such as this one, hinge on your ability to know your target market and create content, products and services which will entice your ideal customer to visit your blog and ultimately, choose your business for their product or service.

CHAPTER 37

Start Your Own Internet Radio Show

Admittedly, this is an advanced strategy, but if you have the willingness to learn new things, then you can implement this strategy into your business and make huge profits from the fame.

While advertising on the radio can be profitable, it can become extremely expensive if you try to increase your marketing campaign too quickly. There is a way to avoid those costs altogether, and become famous too. For the smart business owner, the future of free publicity strategies is internet radio shows. This may come as a total shock to you, but there are internet radio websites which allow you to start your own internet radio show for free. Websites like www.blogtalkradio.com and www.shoutcast.com allow anyone who has a computer and microphone to create their own radio show. This means you can become an overnight star if you have the talent and ability to put together a program and event on a fairly consistent basis.

The benefit of starting your own internet radio show is that you do not have to pay for radio air-time and you can create and air a show as often as you like. You also benefit because you are the one calling the shots and writing the content for your show. This means that you can make it as commercial as you desire, unlike some of the free publicity strategies.

When creating your own radio show, you can schedule the programming to be as long or as short as you see fit. For example, you can create a one hour show which airs once per week or more. You can also script the show to include guest speakers or just simply be built around your business. However, it is in your best interest to create a show that is informative and entertaining because prospects always trying to escape the dull, boring hum of everyday life. If your show can provide that entertainment, then your show will practically be guaranteed to succeed.

The real worth of this strategy is in your ability to get an audience filled with your target market. One of the best ways to do this is by posting a link to your radio show on your own website and on the website of your joint venture partners. You can also post your radio show ad on various other online websites where your target market hangs out.

CHAPTER 38

Highlighting New Products/Services Or Updates Via Vlog

Video blogging is steadily emerging as one of the newest, hottest Internet trends. However, as the art of the video blog – often called "vlogging," "vidding," or "vidblogging" by lovers of the craft – is still relatively new as compared to more traditional methods of information dissemination over the Internet, so many people aren't exactly familiar with the ins and outs of the process.

That's where this primer comes into help. With this in hand, you can go out there and tackle your cyber audiences with the pomp and flash that video blogging offers. The salience of this technique on the Information Superhighway may surprise you. If you've been on the Internet for any period of time at all, you're likely familiar with the blog. A blog – short for "weblog" – is essentially a stream of articles that is constantly being updated. Blogs are used for several purposes across the Internet, from self-promotion to corporate memo slinging to self-expression and nearly anything in between.

Blogs have great value to websites that use them properly – through a blog, a website can both show how active it is as well as reach out constantly to the website's viewers with new, updated information. A blog is often the number one reason why visitors return to certain sites, as most other site content is static. A blog is anything but, and a good blog keeps the viewer wanting more and coming back.

A video blog is the same thing; just replace article feeds with videos. The great thing about video blogging is that it

totally revolutionizes the purpose and scope of a blog –
whereas before the information was consigned to the written
page (rather, the written web page), now the blog has gone 3D.
For example, if you happen to run a travel blog, a traditional
blog would allow you to get the information of your exploits
out to your readers in a concise and timely fashion, but often
your reader's understanding of the situation was limited to both
your writing abilities and the amount of time you had to
dedicate to the creation of the post. Not all of us are
Hemingway – much can get lost in the translation from
experience to memoir. This is where the video blog comes in.
Want your readers to experience the view at the top of
Diamondback? Don't just tell them with words: with the video
blog you can show them with a panoramic shot of the beautiful
island spread at the foot of the mountain.

Video blogging is also incredibly useful for those who run
do-it-yourself websites – instead of dealing with numbering
your steps and agonizing over word choice, why not set up a
camera and film the process of changing a tire, speckling a
wall, or soldering a pipe?

Even if you've never heard of a video blog before, don't
think that this is an isolated phenomenon only known by tech-
heads. The video blog has been in existence since the early
2000s, and one trip to YouTube will show you just how
thriving the video blogging community really is. There's even
an annual video blogging award that's been held since 2006,
and a movie is due to be released as a major motion picture in
2011, which will be comprised entirely of video blogs. Video
blogging is an excellent way of getting the information
regarding your product, services, or opinions out on the
Internet. Just as a traditional blog feed showcases your website
as living entity, the video blog does that and also allows your
face and movements to be connected with the website that's
promoting your goods.

Video blogging truly allows you to bring yourself and your offerings into the homes and workplaces of the viewer like no other form of information sharing can offer. What is video blogging? It's a highly effective way of sharing information through the heightened capabilities of modern technology. Used correctly it can get your name, face, and products out on the world wide web with greater impact and efficiency than any other method of advertising. Why should you video blog? It's effective, inexpensive, and most people would say it's fun!

CHAPTER 39

Marketing Your Business with Online Videos

Video marketing is one of the most effective online marketing strategies, but it's also one of the most advanced strategies for small to medium business owners. The real power of video marketing is its ability to connect your audience to you emotionally and visually. When done correctly, video marketing can reach thousands of prospects in your target market for little to no money out of pocket.

The video marketing campaign strategy involves recording one to three minute videos describing the benefits of your products or services online to hundreds of prospects every day, without actually leaving your business. You can even use a short video to introduce a specific collection and then have the customers view the remainder of the information from your basic website. The best part about video marketing is that you can post your video on popular websites like Youtube.com and begin funneling Youtube.com visitors back to your own website.

Video marketing is the hot thing in online marketing right now. It appeals to many more people who prefer watching videos to get

information than reading. In a culture that grew up on television, video marketing is an ideal way to get the message across. It can also be much more cost effective than using TV advertising, which is too costly for the majority of local businesses to avail of and is a much less targeted form of marketing. Video marketing offers a variety of creative options, including the option of teaching with slides of information being shown while a narrator speaks; pictures that give a great visual being presented to music or an actual video clip that has been produced. In fact you can even do a combination of these types.

Video marketing allows you to:
- give a tour of your facilities
- do demonstrations
- instruct on the use of your products
- solve common problems
- show amazing before and after for services
- give webinars
- share testimonials
- show company overviews
- share expert articles
- deal with questions
- present the company owner in an interview

There are endless uses for video marketing. Because of the visual interest factor, it is useful both onsite and offsite to meet a variety of marketing needs.

- Use to grab the attention of visitors and have them "stick around" your site.
- Many lazy visitors would rather watch a short video than read a bunch of text.
- Use it to brand yourself.
- Use it to build trust.
- Use it to inform or educate visitors.
- Use it offsite to grab searchers and redirect them to your site or phone number.
- Use it to get rankings for multiple keywords or for rankings in suburbs of major metropolitan areas.

Use it to spice up external landing pages.
- Get your business in multiple places.

Creating quality video is not a complicated process, but it does require time and some knowledge.

CHAPTER 40

Mobile Marketing

The next wave of local marketing strategy your business needs to jump on is mobile marketing. Quickly becoming recognized as a mass media channel, marketing to your customers on their mobile devices is now one of the most powerful ways to reach them. Mobile marketing's not a strategy you can just jump in and do, though. Just like any other form of advertising, if it's done poorly, you'll only succeed in irritating your prospective and current customers. Done well, you may be astounded by the results. Currently, one reason mobile marketing is so effective is that the 'open rate' for text messages is nearly 100%. It would be nearly impossible to reach a success rate approaching anywhere near that figure with email marketing or direct mail. Mobile marketing can effectively accomplish these tasks for your business:

- Increase brand awareness
- Gather customer information for marketing purposes
- Draw customers into buying mode more consistently

Some mobile marketing tactics businesses are seeing success with now:

- Polls
- Trivia contests and sweepstakes
- Instant win games
- Free giveaways

- Alerts about sales and other deals
- Graphics and other messages that are so engaging they get forwarded to your customers' contacts

Mobile marketing strategies, like online marketing, are constantly evolving. Be sure if you begin a mobile marketing campaign, that you learn, stay on top of, and follow the rules of the game so you don't inadvertently cause problems for your business.

About The Author

Sahmad Nakumbe's mission is to empower entrepreneurs to beat the odds and enter the Top 1% of Businesses that do over $5 million in annual revenue. Nakumbe has learned a lot about overcoming the odds at a very early age in life. When he was just 12 years old he received a phone call stating that his family had nothing left and later that day found his family's home destroyed by fire. For the next 3 years his family didn't have permanent housing and at some points lived out of a 2-door car. He realized he had a choice, to give up hope and become a statistic or decide that he would do whatever it took to succeed.

Armed with only a strong desire to succeed and help his family, Nakumbe discovered one of his many talents in technology. By 16 he taught himself Web Design and received high school classes on Video Production. His knowledge and success with technology helped him catch the attention of some very successful business executives and at 17, he was named Youth of the Year for the State of Minnesota by the Boys & Girls Club of America. As result he went on to work with Executives at Coca Cola Enterprises. His success did not stop there, Sahmad also was a four sport athlete and all-Section in Football.

Nakumbe has turned his love of technology and passion for helping business owners into a successful digital marketing agency. He is helping small and medium sized companies gain a competitive advantage in the marketplace by leveraging the same tools and technology once only reserves to Fortune 500 companies. Nakumbe specializes in helping these companies get the same results as Fortune 500 companies but at just a small fraction of the investment of those larger companies. The end result is the ability for small and medium sized businesses to overcome the odds of business failure and join the Top 1%.

www.acceleratedmc.com